One World

Where We Live

Valerie Guin

A+
Smart Apple Media

Note
about the series

One World is designed to encourage young readers to learn more about people and places in the wider world. The photographs have been carefully selected to stimulate discussion and comparison.

First published in 2004 by Franklin Watts
96 Leonard Street, London EC2A 4XD

Franklin Watts Australia
45-51 Huntley Street, Alexandria, NSW 2015

This edition published under license from Franklin Watts. All rights reserved.

Copyright © 2004 Franklin Watts.

Editor: Caryn Jenner, Designer: Louise Best, Art director: Jonathan Hair, Map: Ian Thompson
Reading consultant: Hilary Minns, Institute of Education, Warwick University

Acknowledgements: Adrian Arbib/Still Pictures: endpapers, 2, 3, 23. Jo Bass/The Advisory Service for the Education of Travellers, Oxford, 17. Mary Cherry/Holt Studios: 15. James Davis Worldwide: 10. DCLvisions: 11. L. Fordyce/Eye Ubiquitous: 20. David Forman/Eye Ubiquitous: 25. Robert Francis/Hutchison: 19. Ron Giling/Still Pictures: 12. Martin Jones/Ecoscene: 13. Wayne Lawler/Ecoscene: front cover. Roy Maconachie/EASI Images: 16. P. Maurice/Eye Ubiquitous: 7b. John Miles/Eye Ubiquitous: 21. Ray Moller: 7c. Sally Morgan/Ecoscene: 8. Tony Page/Ecoscene: 9. Harmut Schwarzbach/Still Pictures: 6. Ariel Skelley/Corbis: 26. Penny Tweedie/Still Pictures: 22. Julia Waterlow/Eye Ubiquitous: 24, 27. Jim Winkley/Ecoscene: 18. Nick Wiseman/Eye Ubiquitous: 14.

Published in the United States by Smart Apple Media
2140 Howard Drive West, North Mankato, Minnesota 56003

Library of Congress Cataloging-in-Publication Data

Guin, Valerie.
Where we live / by Valerie Guin.
p. cm. — (One world)
ISBN 1-58340-698-0
1. Dwellings—Juvenile literature. 2. Architecture, Domestic—Juvenile literature. I. Title. II. Series: One world (North Mankato, Minn.)

TH4811.5.G85 2005
392.3′6—dc22   2004052505

9 8 7 6 5 4 3 2 1

Contents

5

Our homes

Where you live is your home. Your home keeps you warm and dry. It is somewhere you can eat and sleep—and play!

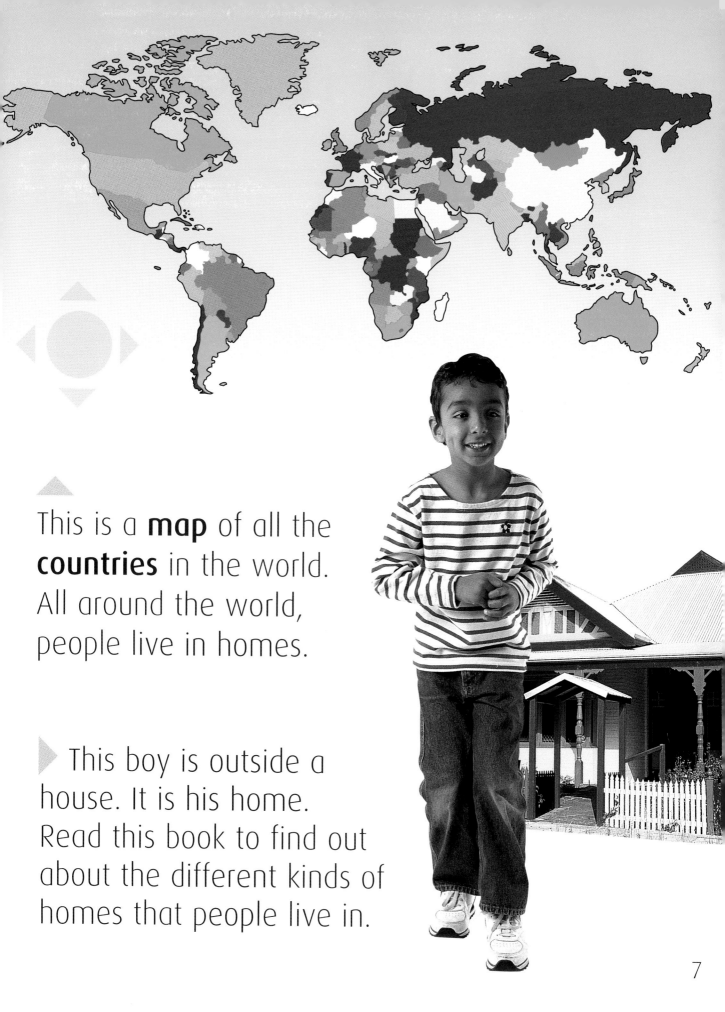

This is a **map** of all the **countries** in the world. All around the world, people live in homes.

▶ This boy is outside a house. It is his home. Read this book to find out about the different kinds of homes that people live in.

Old and new

These old houses are in Italy.
They were built about 900
years ago. Since then, many
people have lived in them.
The insides of the houses
have changed, but the
outsides look much the same.

These houses in Britain were built only a few years ago. The people who live here use new **technology** to recycle the water they use. They also use energy from the sun to make **electricity**.

Wooden houses

In many parts of the world, houses are made of wood. Wood keeps the inside of this house in Switzerland warm and dry in the cold weather.

This house in Indonesia is also made of wood. The sides of the house are open to allow air to pass through and keep the inside cool. The curved roof gives shade from the hot sun.

Apartments

Apartment buildings have many separate homes inside. These colorful apartments are in Argentina.

Tall apartment buildings like these provide homes for the millions of people who live in Hong Kong, a small island in China.

Straw roofs

Roofs can be made of many different **materials**. This thatched cottage in Russia has a roof of straw. The thick straw keeps the house warm.

These houses in Mali also have roofs of straw. Long grass is dried to make the straw. The straw keeps the houses cool and shady.

Decorated homes

People often decorate their homes to make them look special. The women in this village in Burkina Faso worked together to paint these beautiful patterns on their houses.

Traveling families in Britain and Ireland used to live in decorated wagons like this one. This wagon is on display at a traditional traveler fair.

Houseboats

People who live on houseboats can use their homes to **travel** on the water. These houseboats are traveling on a canal in Britain.

In Vietnam, many people live on houseboats like this one. They travel along the **coast** and up and down rivers, carrying goods from one place to another.

Houses on legs

Some houses are raised up on stilts. This house in the United States needs to be high up so the water will go under it rather than into it.

This house is in the
rainforest of Indonesia.
It is up on stilts so the
insects that crawl on the
ground can't get inside.

Living in a tent

These people carry their homes with them as they travel through the hot **desert** in Morocco. Their tents give them shade.

People in the cold mountains of Mongolia also live in tents. To keep warm, they make a fire in the middle of the tent. The smoke goes out through a pipe at the top of the tent, like a chimney.

Living in a cave

In northern China, some homes
are built into the side of cliffs.
The front parts of these houses
are made of brick, with big
windows to let in sunlight.

In places in Tunisia, people dig cave houses down into the ground. Thick stone walls keep the cave houses warm in winter and cool in summer.

A house is a home

In many homes, families gather together to eat. This family in the United States sits at the kitchen table to have its meal.

This family gathers outside
its home to eat its meal.
The family lives in Egypt,
where the weather is hot
and dry.

All around the world

All over the world, people relax together at home.

United States

Tunisia —

Morocco —

Argentina

The countries that you have read about are shown in pink on this map of the world. Find the country that matches each picture in the book.

Ireland

Switzerland

Mongolia

Britain

Russia

Italy

Egypt

China

Vietnam

Mali

Indonesia

Burkina Faso

Glossary

coast where the land meets the sea

countries places with their own governments

desert an area of land that is very dry

electricity a kind of power that can be used to work lights and machines

map a drawing that shows us where to find places

materials things used to make other things

rainforest a kind of forest in a very warm, rainy place

technology using science to make useful inventions

travel to move from one place to another

Index

30